High Noon

Wild Bill Hickok and the Code of the Old West

Eric Fein

ROSEN CENTRAL
PRIMARY SOURCE™

THE ROSEN PUBLISHING GROUP, INC., NEW YORK

Published in 2004 by The Rosen Publishing Group, Inc.
29 East 21st Street, New York, NY 10010

Editor: Shira Laskin
Book Design: Layla Sun
Photo Researcher: Rebecca Anguin-Cohen
Series Photo Researcher: Jeff Wendt

Photo Credits: Cover (left), pp. 14, 30 Library of Congress, Rare Book and Special Collections Division; cover (right)
illustration © Debra Wainwright/The Rosen Publishing Group; title page, p. 10 Springfield-Greene County Library,
Springfield, MO; p. 6 Kansas State Historical Society; p. 18 Michael Glenn/Springfield-Greene County Library;
pp. 22, 29 Greene County Archives and Records Center; p. 31 Wyoming State Archives; p. 32 © SuperStock, Inc.

First Edition

Library of Congress Cataloging-in-Publication Data

Fein, Eric.
    High noon : Wild Bill Hickok and the code of the Old West / Eric
    Fein.— 1st ed.
    p. cm. — (Great moments in American history)
    Summary: In Springfield, Missouri, in 1865, Wild Bill Hickok has a
    shootout with an old adversary over a question of honor.
    ISBN 0-8239-4390-9 (lib. bdg.)
    1. Hickok, Wild Bill, 1837-1876—Juvenile literature. 2. Tutt, Davis,
    d. 1865—Juvenile literature. 3.
    Violence—Missouri—Springfield—History—19th century—Juvenile
    literature. 4. Springfield (Mo.)--Biography—Juvenile literature. 5.
    West (U.S.)—Biography—Juvenile literature. 6. Frontier and pioneer
    life—Missouri—Springfield—Juvenile literature. 7. Frontier and
    pioneer life—West (U.S.)—Juvenile literature. [1. Hickok, Wild Bill,
    1837-1876. 2. Tutt, Davis, d. 1865. 3. Frontier and pioneer
    life—Missouri. 4. Springfield (Mo.)—History—19th century.] I. Title.
    II. Series.

    F594.H62F45 2004
    977.8'78—dc21

                                                        2003007572

Manufactured in the United States of America

Contents

Preface

*J*ames Butler "Wild Bill" Hickok was born on May 27, 1837, in Homer, Illinois. He held many different jobs in his life. However, Hickok was *best* known for his skills with a gun. He could draw and shoot with perfect aim.

Hickok became a Western legend in 1861. He had been working as a stagecoach driver on the Santa Fe and Oregon Trails. One day, Hickok was attacked and wounded by a bear. While he healed, he was sent to do light work at the Rock Creek Station in Nebraska. There, a man named Dave McCanles and a few of his friends started trouble with Hickok. There was a shoot-out. When it was over, Hickok was the only man left alive.

Most people who have studied what happened agree that McCanles and his friends started the fight. Hickok had no choice but to kill them in

order to save his own life. However, when the news reached the East, it caused quite a stir. Newspapers and magazines printed twisted accounts of what had happened. Some said that Hickok had fought off ten men and was a wild killer. This was the first of many stories that were told about Hickok's life. The stories made him seem like a heartless killer. Hickok became the subject of books and magazine stories. People believed he shot and killed over one hundred men in his life—when he probably really killed ten.

During 1864 and 1865, Hickok spent time in Springfield, Missouri, where he worked as a scout for the Union army during the American Civil War. After the war, he decided to stay in Springfield. This decision led him to another shoot-out—one that made him even more famous as a wild killer. It was a decision he would come to regret. . . .

Hickok was known for his skills with a gun as a young man. He often practiced shooting targets behind his family's farm in Illinois.

Chapter One

Wild Bill in Springfield

T he Lyon Inn was a hotel about a block from the town square in Springfield, Missouri. Wild Bill Hickok had been living there since the end of the Civil War in the spring of 1865. He had worked as a scout in the Union army. Like many men who had finished their army service, Hickok wanted to rest. Springfield seemed like the perfect place to do just that. It was full of saloons and gambling, and Hickok loved to drink and play cards.

People in Springfield lived by the code of the West. This was a set of unspoken, unwritten rules that ran life in many western towns. The code was built on honor and respect. If a person's honor or respect was questioned, things could become dangerous. Hickok didn't know it, but his honor would be tested that summer in Springfield.

On a July morning, Hickok stood in the town square with his friend, Captain Richard Bentley Owen. Hickok was over 6 feet tall and towered over Owen. No one wanted to start trouble with Hickok.

Hickok pulled out his prized pocket watch. He saw it was time for breakfast. He and Owen walked through town. Owen teased Hickok about all of the gambling he was doing. Owen thought Hickok should get a real job. However, Hickok just wanted to have fun.

A group of young boys stood on the side of the street. They whispered to each other and pointed toward Hickok as he and Owen walked by. One of the boys called out to Hickok.

"Hey, Wild Bill! Shoot anyone today?" asked the boy while his friends laughed. They had dared the boy to talk to Hickok.

Hickok stopped walking and turned toward the boys. They were now silent—and scared.

"Why would you ask me such a question?" Hickok asked.

The boys were too scared to speak. Finally, one of them said, "We've heard stories about what you did at Rock Creek. People say you killed ten men in the blink of an eye. They say you're a cold-blooded killer!"

Hickok shook his head. There were many stories about the shoot-out with Dave McCanles at Rock Creek. It upset Hickok that people thought he was a heartless killer. He wished that people didn't believe every story they read in the newspapers. He wanted people to know that he had killed those men in self-defense. The rumors about Hickok's wild nature troubled him.

"Come on, Bill," said Owen. The two men left the boys and continued walking. They reached the other end of the square and turned the corner. Hickok stopped and stared down the road. There stood a man that Hickok had not seen in a long time.

The hair on the back of Hickok's neck stood straight up. The man was Davis Tutt—and Hickok knew he was trouble.

This photograph of Springfield's town square was taken in the early 1860s—only a few years before the Hickok-Tutt shoot-out marked its place in history.

Chapter Two

Trouble With Tutt

T he next day, Hickok was sitting at a table in the Lyon Inn. Tutt came into the hotel and walked up to Hickok.

"It's been a while, Bill," said Tutt. Hickok smoothed his mustache with his long fingers and slowly looked up at Tutt. He leaned back in his chair with his hands at his sides, near his guns.

"Good day," said Hickok without a hint of friend-liness. "I guess it has been about two years now." The men stared each other down. There was quite a history between them. They had both fought in the Civil War, but for different sides. They had gambled together and even done business together. Years earlier, Hickok had bought a horse from Tutt. The two men were friends at the time and it didn't bother Tutt that Hickok had forgotten to pay him.

There were other problems between the men that made them hate each other. Springfield was a small town where rumors spread quickly. One of the rumors the townspeople spoke of was about Hickok and Tutt's sister. It was said that Hickok cared for her very much and spent time with her, even though the Tutt family had asked him to stay away. Another story suggested that Tutt had stolen a girlfriend of Hickok's while Hickok was away. No one in the town knew for sure if either story was true. What they *did* know was that Springfield was probably not big enough for both Hickok *and* Tutt.

Hickok stood up from the table to face Tutt and asked, "Visiting Springfield?"

Tutt smiled. He knew Hickok was trying to make him feel unwelcome in the town. "No, Bill. I'm looking for work. I'm moving my family here," said Tutt.

Hickok calmly said, "Are you sure that's a wise thing to do?"

Tutt was not going to let Hickok scare him out of moving to town. Tutt knew the best way to bother Hickok, too. Hickok was a man of pride who *never* turned down a poker game.

"Still a gambling man, Bill?" asked Tutt with an evil grin.

"What do you have in mind?" said Hickok as he took a sip of his drink.

"Just a friendly game of poker. If I remember, that's your game," said Tutt.

Hickok did indeed have plans to play in a poker game that night. He knew inviting Tutt to play might be a bad idea. Yet Hickok never turned down a game—or a challenge. Hickok reached for his prized watch to check the time. He told Tutt to meet him back at the Lyon Inn in a few hours. Then he put the watch back in his pocket. Tutt stared at the watch and then smiled at Hickok.

"I'll see you tonight, Bill," said Tutt as he left. Hickok didn't know it, but Tutt planned to take all of his money to settle their past.

This drawing of the poker game at the Lyon Inn was done by A. R. Waud. It was printed in the February 1867 issue of *Harper's New Monthly Magazine*. Hickok sits at the table holding cards and Tutt stands, having just taken Hickok's pocket watch.

Chapter Three

A Dangerous Game

That night, July 20, 1865, the Lyon Inn was home to a very tense poker game. Everyone had heard the rumors and knew about the bad feelings between Hickok and Tutt. The townspeople feared the game might start trouble.

Tutt arrived at the inn. Hickok and the other players were already seated around the poker table. There was an empty chair waiting for Tutt. He nodded to the other players, ready to start the game. Tutt had lost to Hickok in the past and didn't want to lose again. Tutt wanted to win all of Hickok's money—and to make him look like a fool in front of the townspeople.

However, the game did not go as Tutt planned. He grew angrier as Hickok won round after round. Tutt's money was quickly disappearing.

15

"This isn't right!" shouted Tutt as he slammed down another losing hand on the table. Everyone's poker chips jumped.

Hickok's eyes narrowed into slits as he looked at Tutt over his cards. "What's the problem, Tutt?" said Hickok.

"You know what the problem is," said Tutt. "You're taking my money while you never paid me the money you owe me! Remember the horse?"

Hickok thought for a moment and realized Tutt was right. He *had* forgotten to pay for the horse. Hickok was a man of honor, and didn't want to owe money to anyone. He would pay Tutt the money for the horse. "Fair enough," said Hickok. He pushed some money across the table to Tutt.

"That's not enough," yelled Tutt, now red in the face. "You also owe me money from our last poker game."

Hickok shook his head. Tutt was wrong.

"If I owe you anything, Tutt, it is for the horse. That's all. Now take the money and let's get back to this game," Hickok said as he checked his watch. It was getting late.

Instead of taking the money, Tutt grabbed Hickok's prized watch. "Well, if you won't pay me, I'll just have to take this," said Tutt. Hickok shot up out of his chair. His hands hung by his sides, just inches from his guns. The other players nervously backed away from the table.

"Put down the watch," said Hickok. His voice was barely above a whisper. The room was silent. Everyone was thinking the same thing: *Would Hickok go for his guns?*

Tutt laughed, spun the watch by its chain, and dropped it into his pocket. He knew Hickok wouldn't draw his guns in the hotel. There were too many people around. Tutt turned and left, tipping his hat as he walked through the door. Hickok was very angry.

Davis Tutt
Born 1839
In Yellville, Arkansas
Died July 21, 1865
on the public square
in Springfield, Missouri

After the shoot-out, Davis Tutt was buried in Springfield. The back of his headstone presents the story of the gunfight and has pictures of Hickok's pocket watch, playing cards, and a gun.

Chapter Four

Shoot-out in Springfield

When Hickok woke up the next morning, he was still angry about what had happened the night before. He dressed and sat on his bed while he cleaned and reloaded his guns before leaving for the day. Hickok always took good care of his guns. He wanted them to be perfect in case he had to defend himself.

There was a knock at his door. It was Captain Owen. Owen had been at the Lyon Inn the night before. He had seen everything that happened. He knew that Hickok was embarrassed when Tutt walked out with the watch. Owen knew that Tutt had challenged Hickok's honor. Owen also knew that there were rumors going around Springfield that morning that would make Hickok even angrier.

"Bill," he said, "you better get down to the square. Rumor has it that Tutt is going to be there around noon. He's going to wear your watch in front of the whole town."

Hickok was outraged.

Owen continued, "That's not all, Bill. People are saying Tutt's looking for a fight." Hickok stood up slowly and placed his guns on his belt. As always, the guns faced back with their handles pointing forward. This allowed Hickok to spin them up and out of his gun belt very quickly. Hickok put on his hat and the two men left the room. They ate and then headed to the town square.

It was nearly noon and the hot, summer sun blazed down on Springfield. The square was crowded with townspeople. Hickok could see Tutt. The rumors Owen heard were true. Tutt was wearing the watch for all to see. Hickok stood on one side of the square and Tutt stood on the other. As their eyes finally met, the crowd became silent.

Hickok called out to Tutt. He warned him not to cross the square wearing the watch. Tutt ignored Hickok and slowly started to walk toward him.

Suddenly, Tutt drew his gun. In a split second, Hickok spun his own gun out and took aim at Tutt. *CRACK!* Both men fired at the exact same moment, each sending a bullet flying toward the other.

Tutt fell to the ground. Hickok's bullet had hit him in the heart. Hickok stood untouched. Tutt had missed his mark.

People gathered around Tutt's lifeless body. His friends were very upset and screamed that Hickok was a murderer. Hickok pointed his gun at them and warned them to stop.

The town's sheriff was called to the scene. He arrived shortly and looked at Tutt lying dead on the ground. Hickok dropped his guns. He knew what was coming.

The sheriff approached Hickok and placed him under arrest.

THE STATE OF MISSOURI TO

John F. McMahan

YOU are hereby commanded to be and appear before the Honorable Judge of our _Greene_

Circuit Court, at the Court House in the town of _Springfield_, in said county, on

the _instant_ _this_ day of the next term of said Court, which will commence on the _____

Monday after the _Second_ Monday in _July_ , A. D. 186 _5_

then and there to testify and the truth to speak in a cause then and there pending, wherein _____

The State of Missouri

_____ Plaintiff , and _____

James Hickok

_____ Defendant , on the part of the said _State_

_____

Hereof fail not, under the penalty of the law.

IN TESTIMONY WHEREOF, I, _Robert_

A McMack Clerk of our said Cir-

cuit Court, have hereunto set my hand and affixed the seal

of said court, at Office, in the town of _Spring_

field , this _5_ day of

August , A. D. 186 _5_

R A McMack Clerk.

By W L Mack D C

Many people who had seen the shoot-out went to Hickok's trial to tell the judge and jury what happened. Each person received an official notice, such as the one above, ordering them to appear in count.

Chapter Five

Wild Bill on Trial

*H*ickok was charged with manslaughter. It was believed that he had not planned to shoot Tutt, but was to blame for Tutt's death. Hickok was put on trial in August 1865. A jury would decide if he should go to jail. Many townspeople came to the trial to see what would happen. Some were quite angry that such a shoot-out could take place in Springfield. Some believed Hickok was a murderer and wanted to see him put behind bars.

Many people who were in the town square on the day of the shoot-out were called to the court to tell the judge and jury what had happened. Not all of the stories they told about that day were true. The jury had to decide who was telling the truth.

Tutt's friends claimed that Tutt had been out in the square just minding his own business when Hickok shot him. They wanted the jury to believe Hickok was a cold-blooded killer and that the shoot-out was entirely his fault.

The owner of the Lyon Inn and some of the poker players from the game the night before the shoot-out spoke as well. They explained what happened at the poker game. They told the jury that Tutt had taken the watch and was looking for trouble with Hickok.

Next, other people who had seen the shoot-out spoke. They told the same story: Tutt drew his gun and shot first. After hearing this, the judge asked the sheriff to bring in Tutt's gun. They carefully looked at the gun. There was one bullet missing inside, proving that Tutt had fired the gun at Hickok.

After everyone had spoken, the jury thought about the case. They had to decide if Hickok had purposely killed Tutt—or if Tutt had pulled out his gun first. If Tutt had done so,

they could believe Hickok had to shoot Tutt to save his own life.

The judge called for a decision. The jury found Hickok not guilty. They believed he had shot Tutt in self-defense. Hickok was a free man.

The town of Springfield had mixed feelings about the decision to set Hickok free. Those close to Hickok were glad he was a free man. They knew the truth about that day in the square. They also knew the rumors about Hickok being a heartless killer were not true.

Some people in the town were angry. Tutt's friends were very upset. Others were scared. They didn't want shoot-outs in Springfield. They also felt that *someone* should have to go to jail for Tutt's death. These people were angry that Hickok was set free. They called him a killer even more than they had before.

After a few months, Hickok left Springfield. With all of the stories about his past, and the shoot-out with Tutt, Hickok felt out of

place there. He was unhappy about people's reactions to the shoot-out. It was time to move on.

Hickok would take part in many more shoot-outs. He was finally murdered by John "Jack" McCall in South Dakota in 1876. Stories of his skills with a gun had followed him everywhere he went. Hickok hated these stories. He told people that while he had taken lives, it was only to save his own.

The story of the shoot-out between Hickok and Tutt in Springfield's town square became very famous. It was the first gunfight of its kind recorded in history. Many Western movies and TV shows used the events of that day as a model for their stories: At high noon, two men walk toward each other across a crowded square in a small town. Both men pull their guns and shoot, each with the chance of losing his life.

Hickok's shot that day in Springfield didn't just hit the heart of a man named Tutt—it hit the heart of the American West and left its mark.

Glossary

gambling (GAM-buhl-ing) betting money on the outcome of a race, a game, or something that might happen

jury (JU-ree) a group of people at a trial that listens to the facts and decides whether the person accused of a crime is innocent or guilty

legend (LEJ-uhnd) a person who has many stories told about himself or herself that are not always true

manslaughter (MAN-slaw-tur) the crime of killing someone without intending to do so

poker (POH-kur) a card game in which players bet something of value, such as money

regret (ri-GRET) to be sad or sorry about something

rumor (ROO-mur) something said by many people although it may not be true

self-defense (SELF-di-fenss) the act of protecting yourself against attacks or threats

saloon (suh-LOON) a bar where people can buy and drink alcoholic beverages

scout (SKOUT) someone sent to find out and bring back information

trial (TRYE-uhl) the examination of evidence in a court of law to decide if a charge or claim is true

Primary Sources

We can learn about the people, places, and events of Hickok's time by looking for the right clues. These clues can be found in old documents, letters, diaries, paintings, and photographs. For example, in February 1867, *Harper's New Monthly Magazine* printed a story about Hickok which twisted the truth about his gunfights. From this story, shown on page 30, we learn the writer's point of view about Hickok. The writer claimed Hickok was a wild man who killed many more men that he really had. From this story, we can learn about how Hickok became a legend.

Primary sources can also help us reconstruct different parts of Hickok's life. By analyzing his grave on page 32, we learn that Hickok was killed by a man named Jack McCall. McCall shot Hickok in the head while Hickok was playing poker in Deadwood, South Dakota. Sources such as the magazine article and Hickok's grave give us clues to help us understand parts of Hickok's life.

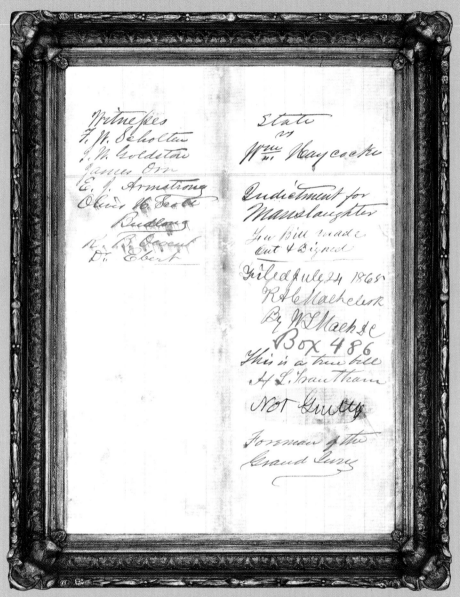

Before the jury gave their decision at Hickok's trial, the judge carefully explained that people have the right to defend themselves. Above is the jury's decision. It lists their names and, at the bottom, reads "not guilty."

HARPER'S
NEW MONTHLY MAGAZINE.

No. CCI.—FEBRUARY, 1867.—Vol. XXXIV.

WILD BILL.

SEVERAL months after the ending of the | of extensive dimensions, yet it is the largest in
civil war I visited the city of Springfield in | that part of the State, and all roads lead to it—
Southwest Missouri. Springfield is not a burgh | which is one reason why it was the *point d'ap-*

Entered according to Act of Congress, in the year 1867, by Harper and Brothers, in the Clerk's Office of the
District Court for the Southern District of New York.

Vol. XXXIV.—No. 201.—T

In February 1867, *Harper's New Monthly Magazine* featured an interview between writer George W. Nichols and Hickok. This article helped create Hickok's image as a cold-blooded killer. This illustration of Hickok was done by artist A. R. Waud. It was printed on the cover of the magazine.

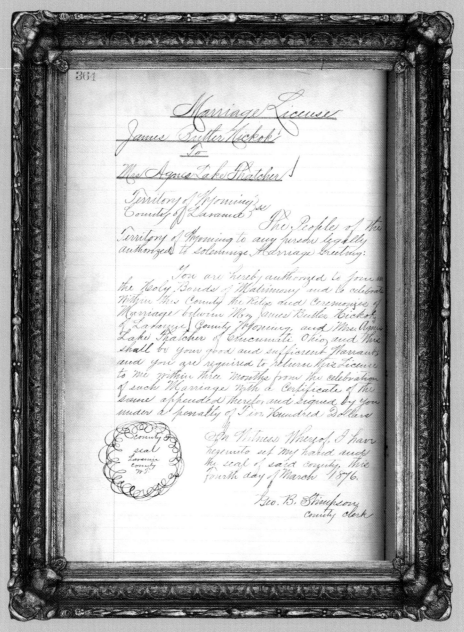

Hickok married Agnes Thatcher Lake, a circus performer, on March 5, 1876. Shortly after their honeymoon, Hickok traveled to Deadwood, South Dakota. He hoped to find gold and bring his new bride out West. Five months later, however, Hickok was killed. Above is the couple's marriage license.

Hickok was murdered by Jack McCall while playing poker on August 2, 1876. Hickok's friend, Charlie Utter, arranged to have this headstone placed in front of the grave. Utter, known to Hickok as "Colorado Charlie," was a hunter and trapper.

DATE DUE

FEB 73			
MAR 11			
NOV 1			
			Printed in USA

HIGHSMITH #45230